Tree Watching vol 0.

_X	[You Are Here]
_0-1	This is what your life could look like if you bought like a billion stickers
_2-55	Illustrations
_56+	Index

Thank you to the /r/trees community for being such a great and welcoming place, to everyone that shares their fantastic photos there, and to my friends and family.

Get your art hot and fresh out of the marker!

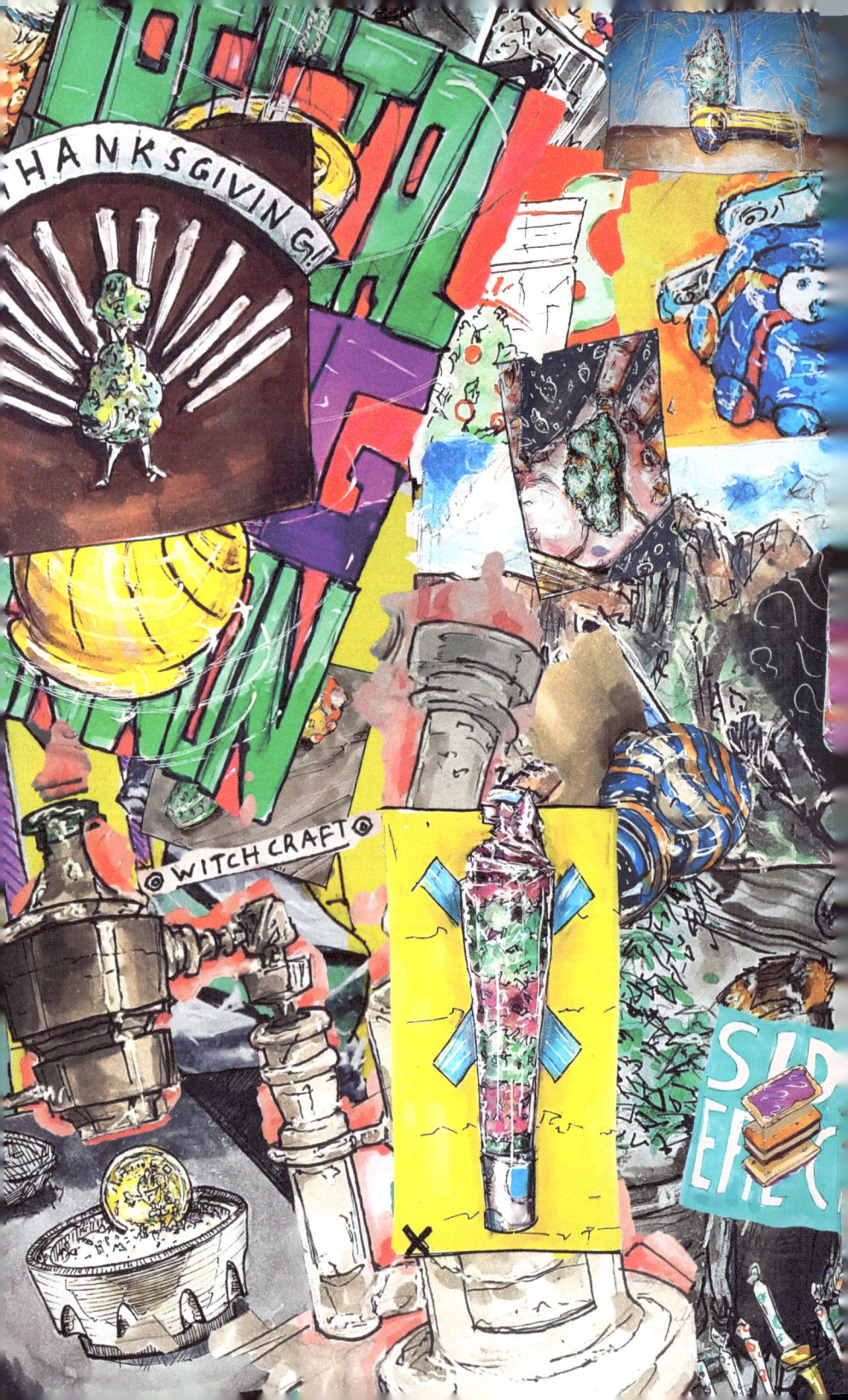

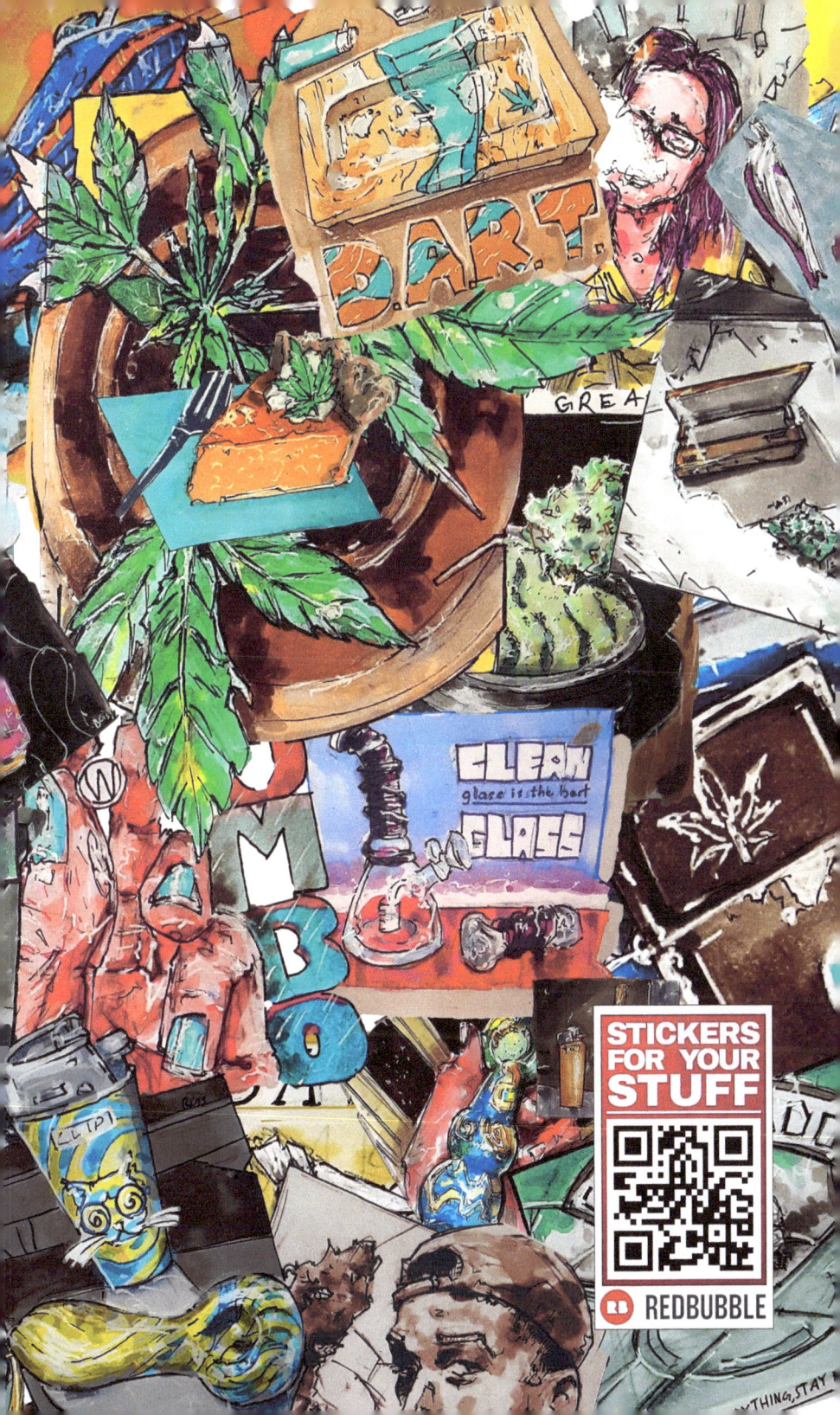

-Tree Watching vol.0-

GDP/LJ

▲982 Decided to make a striped joint with some GDP and Lavender Jones! Inspired from a post I saw a little while back.
-/u/MNpatient420

EARLY CHRISTMAS

▲794 Christmas trees in November
-/u/sk8_ark

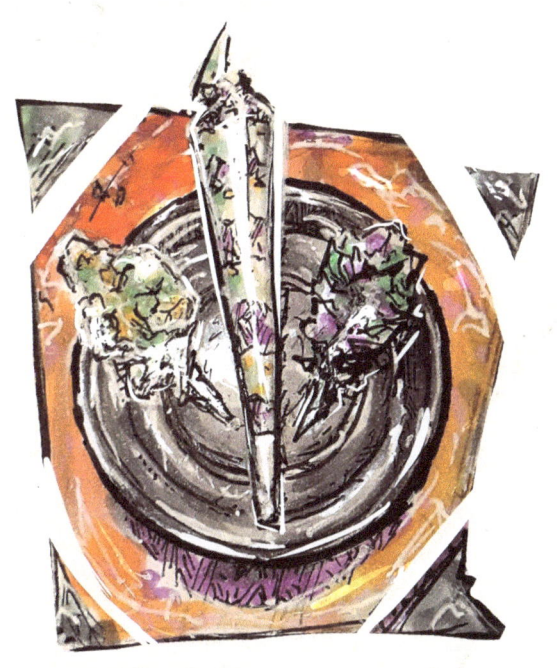

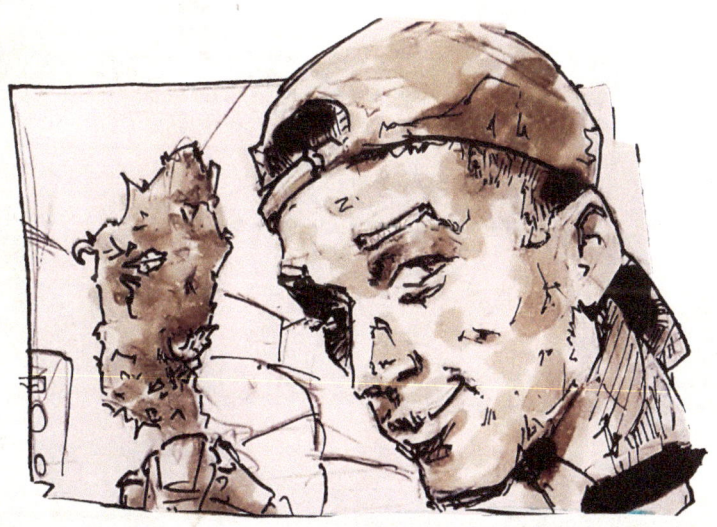

-Tree Watching vol.0-

▲13.9K The lethal side effects of smoking Marihuana
-/u/TheRealErls

▲55 Jingle bells
-/u/uncorroboratedcow

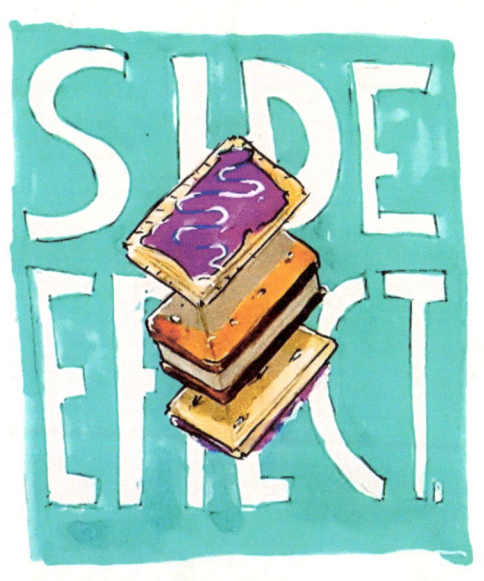

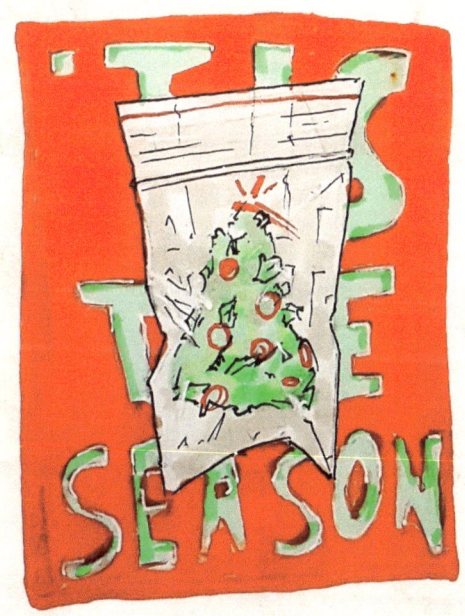

JAMBI

▲129 I thought my new piece looked pretty dope. I named it Jambi
-/u/▮▮▮▮▮▮▮

THICC

▲19 Got a new thicc boi
-/u/TrentdelaCruz

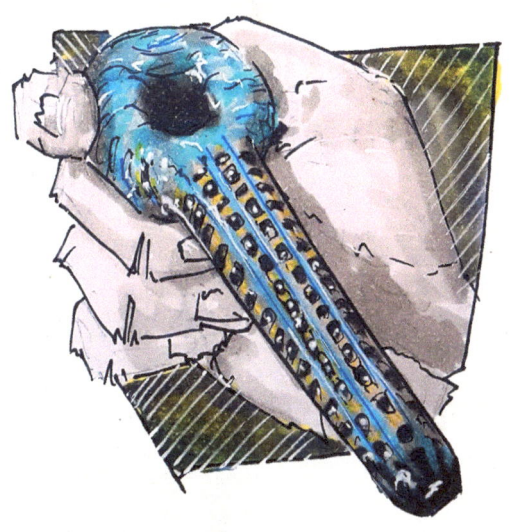
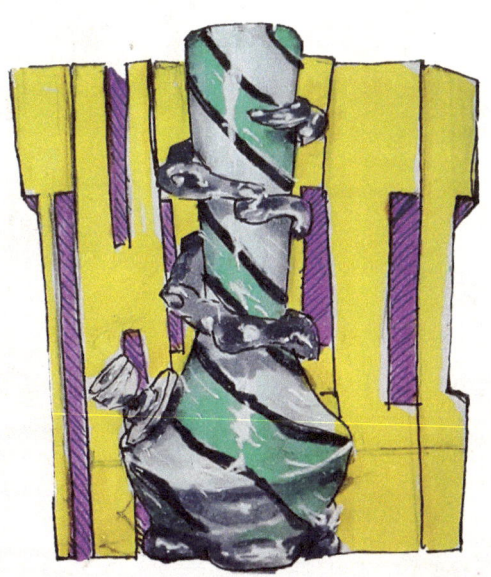

-Tree Watching vol.0-

D.A.R.T.

▲1.1K I made a dope ass rolling tray.
-/u/

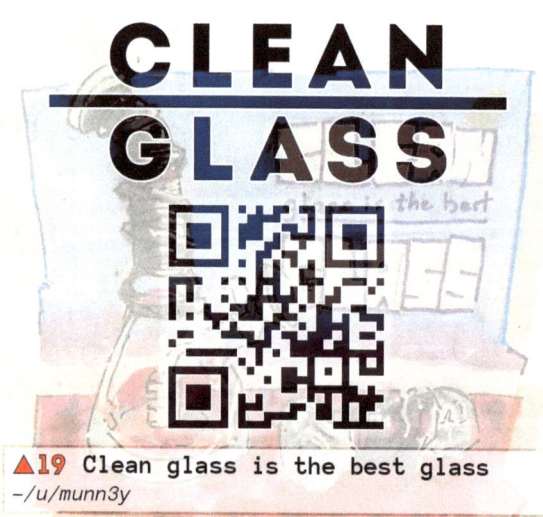

CLEAN GLASS

▲19 Clean glass is the best glass
-/u/munn3y

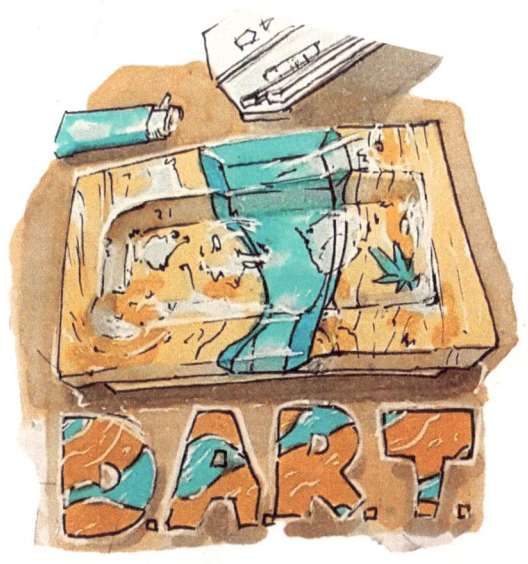

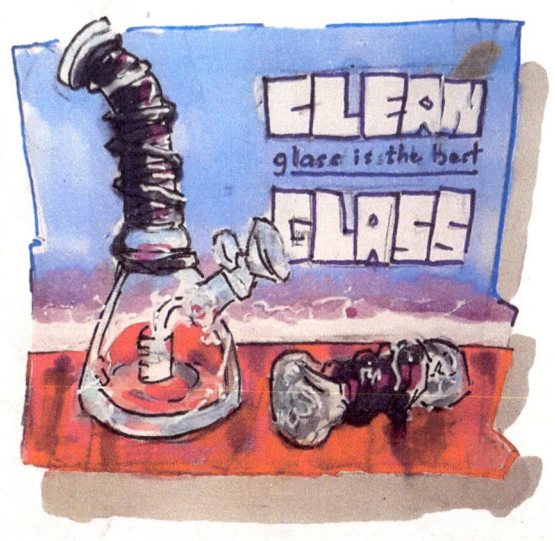

-Tree Watching vol.0-

▲49 Thanks for the great recommendation trees! My buddy and I found a great weed cafe in Amsterdam
-/u/keeganwells3

▲1.5K A true zen garden.
-/u/

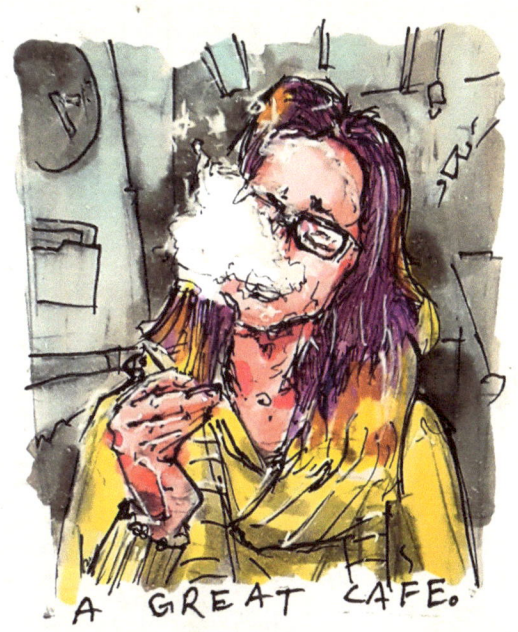

A GREAT CAFE.

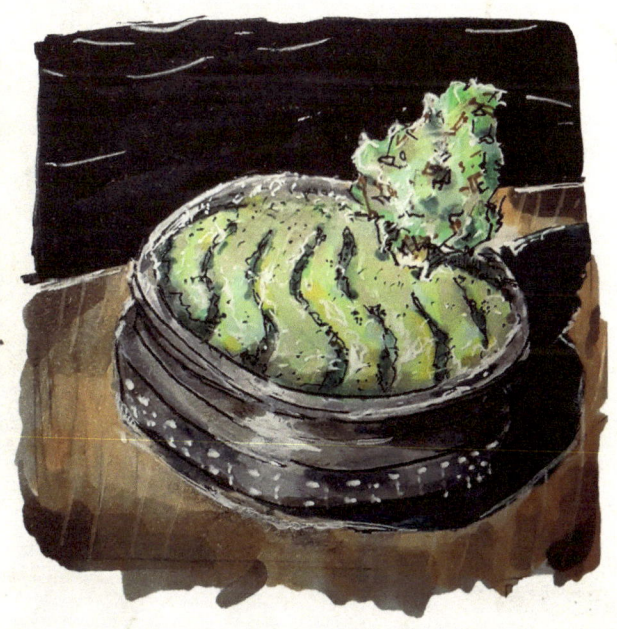

-Tree Watching vol.0-

▲37 Excited to introduce you (and in a moment myself) to Eureka!
-/u/ghosthostjbo

▲547 I don't partake myself but my mother does, recently I found her smoking out of an aluminum foil pipe. I immediately went down to our local headshop and got her a new pipe just in time for her 55th birthday.
-/u/BurritoBanditos

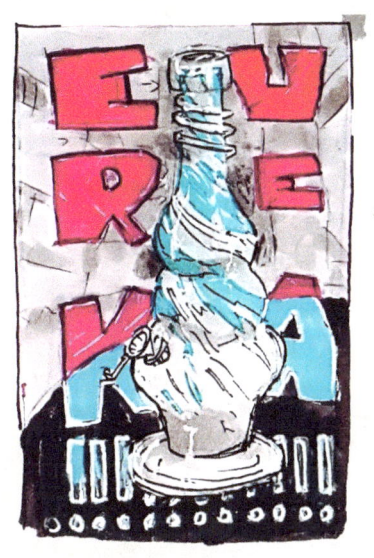
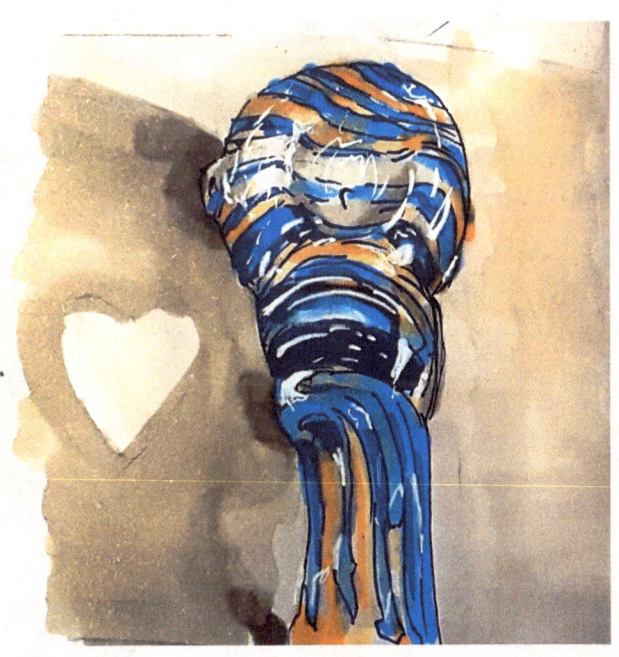

-Tree Watching vol.0-

▲72 "Load captain Solo Dolo into the cargo hold".
-/u/murknmurda

▲52 Ready to medicate on the go!
-/u/

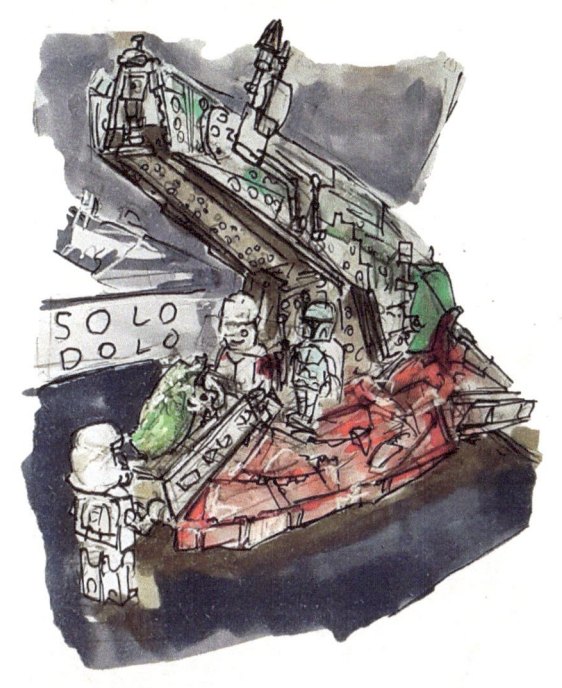

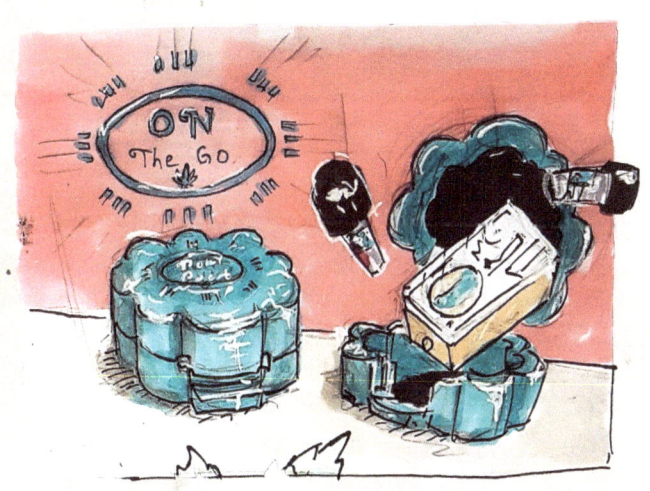

—Tree Watching vol.0—

FIRST GROW

🔺3 My 1st attempt!
-/u/▮▮▮▮▮▮▮▮

PERFECT PAIR

🔺14 My first attempt at this
-/u/Vincent_Veganja

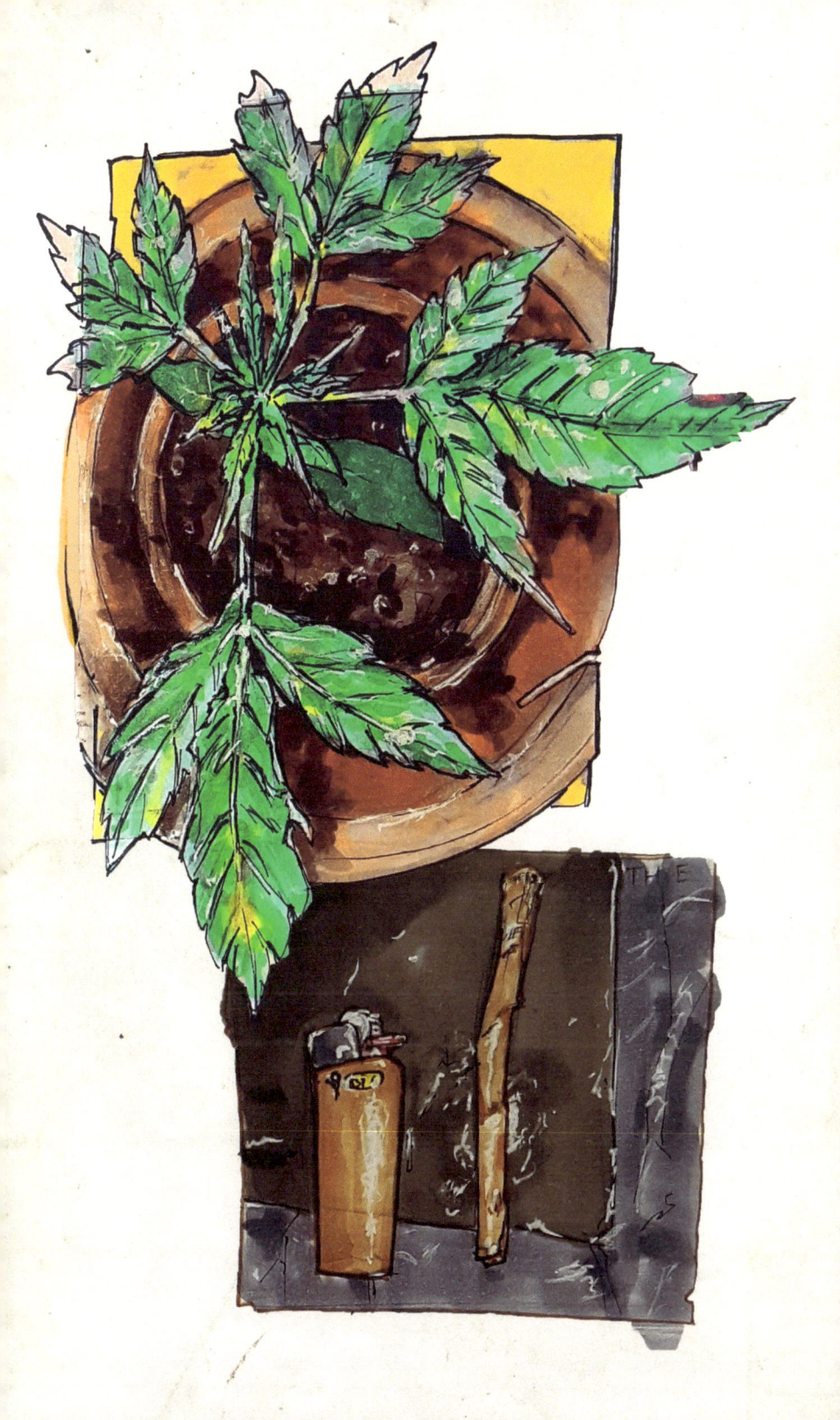

—Tree Watching vol.0—

WITCH CRAFT

▲563 On the east coast, dabbing is still relatively 'new and rare'. Basically witchcraft to most of my friends!
–/u/__Ratatoskr__

GARDEN VARIETY

▲342 When the only papers you have are of the garden-variety
–/u/

ATLANTEAN BEETLE

▲25 Having a toke and thinking about how I wanna ask this girl out [6]
–/u/a7xwarrior

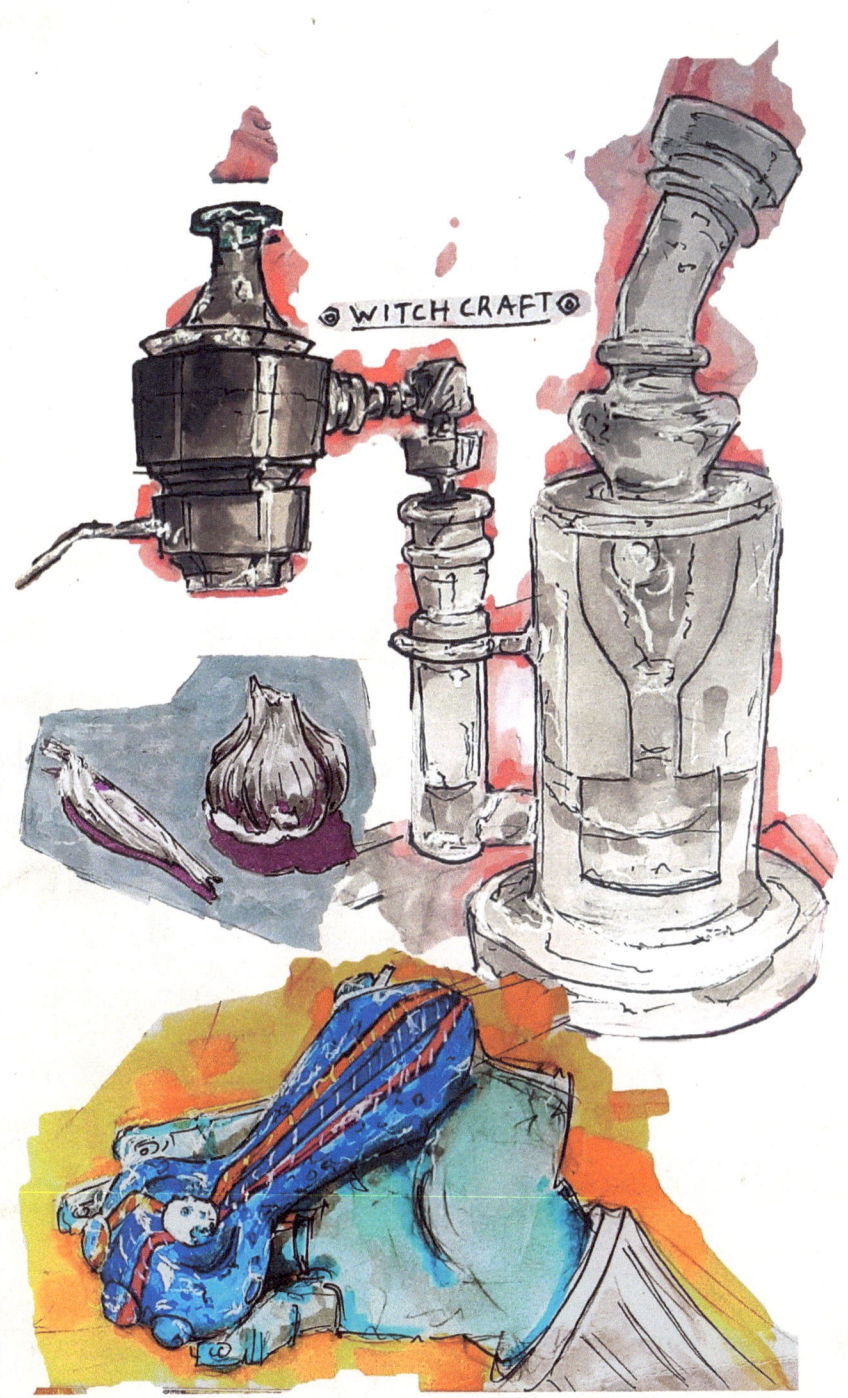

—Tree Watching vol.0—

HAPPY
THANKSGIVING

▲8.2K [REPOST] Happy Thanksgiving to all of you! This is my turkey of choice for today!
-/u/▬▬▬▬▬▬▬

DESSERT

▲553 Happy Thanksgiving to all the ents!
-/u/▬▬▬▬▬▬▬

BAKE THE
TURKEY

▲282 Happy Danksgiving! Everyone enjoy their turkey and be grateful... I know I am
-/u/GoonSquad69420

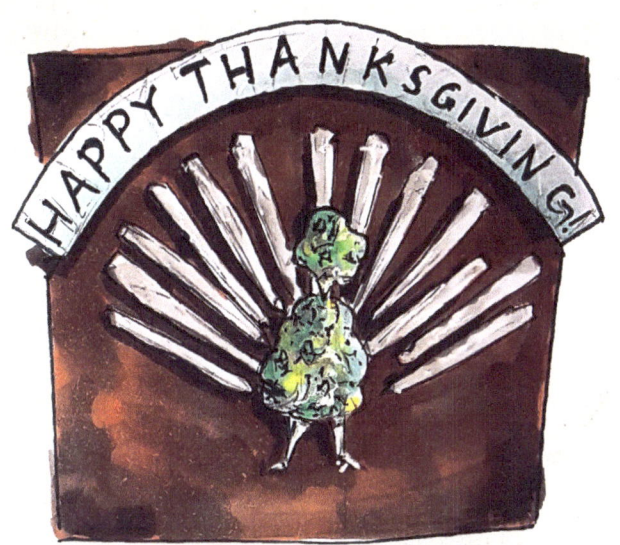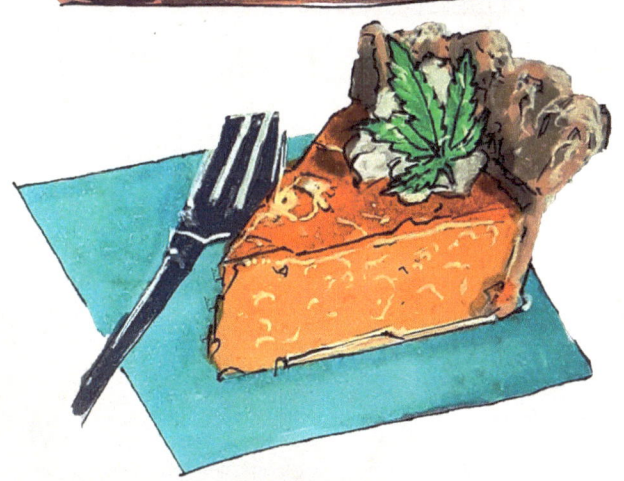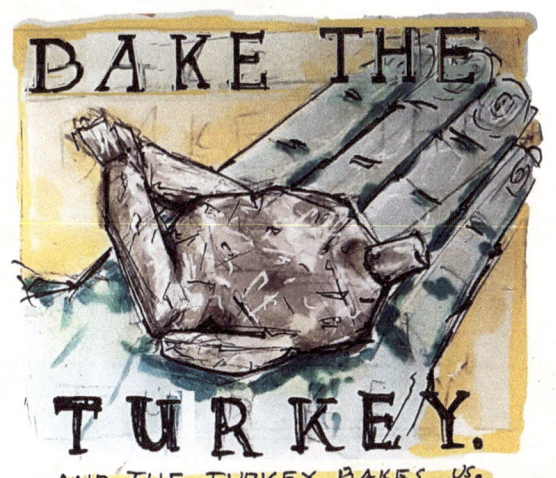

-Tree Watching vol.0-

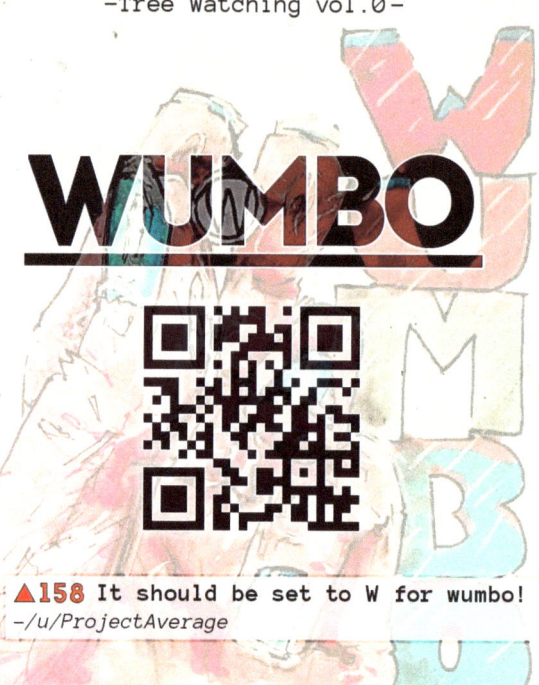

▲158 It should be set to W for wumbo!
-/u/ProjectAverage

▲79 Cheers, guys
-/u/kisse5

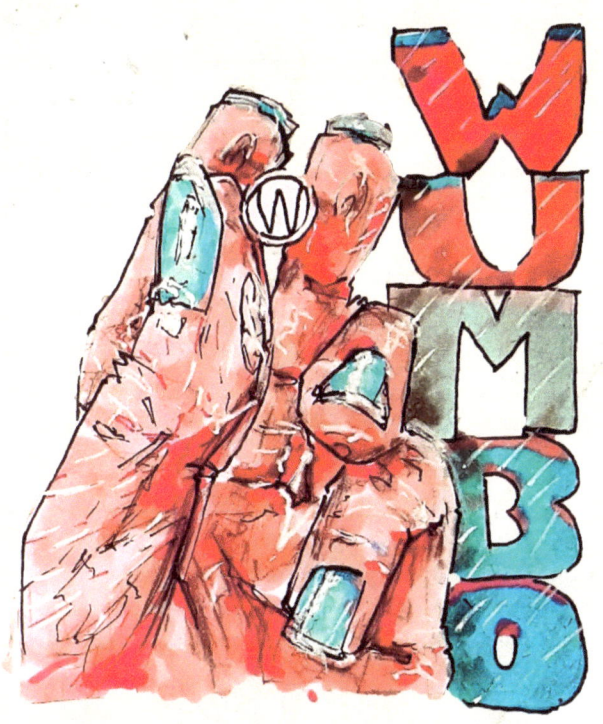
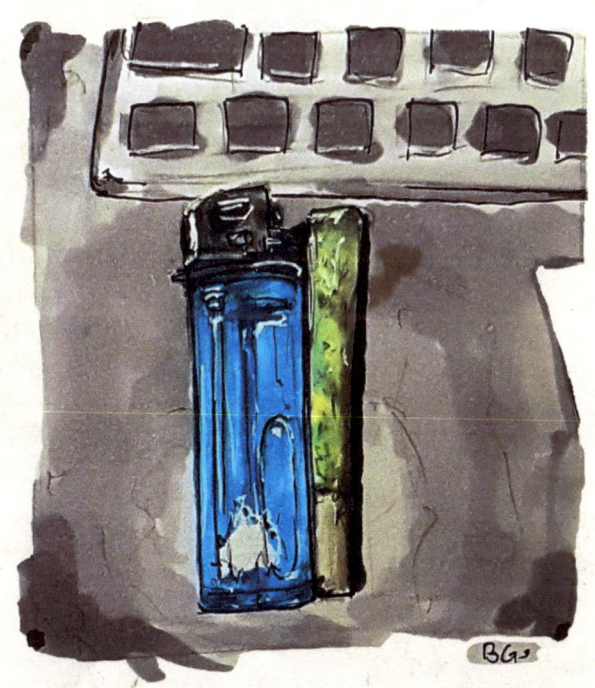

—Tree Watching vol.0—

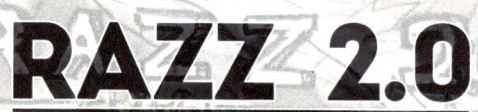

🔺103 Razz 2.0 a strain we saved from extinction at our shop.
–/u/Baconbeatseverything

🔺223 She's a bad bitch.
–/u/

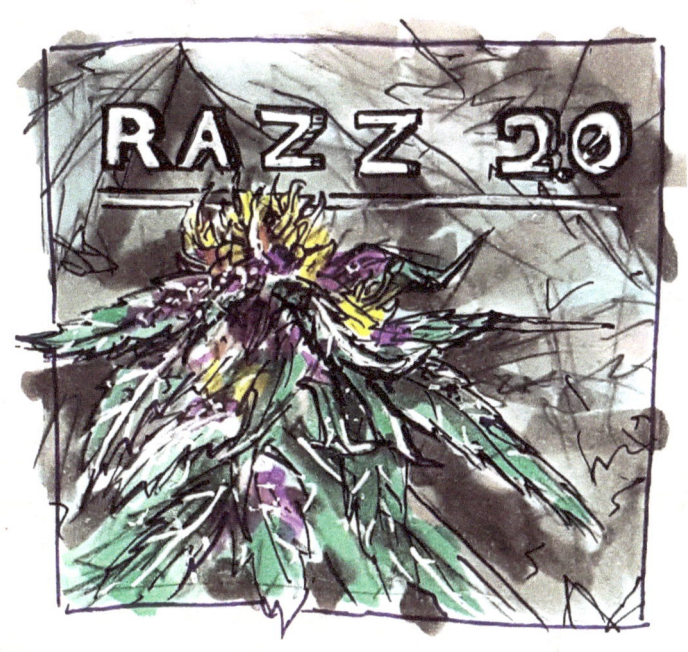
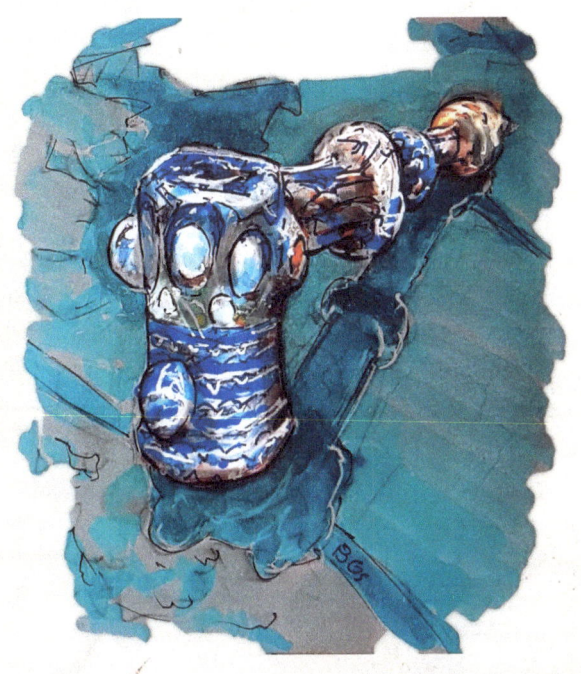

—Tree Watching vol.0—

▲5 new baby needs a name
-/u/theTiki_LBJ

▲102 Tomorrow it's back to the grind for the last two weeks of the semester. One last round for the holidays!
-/u/

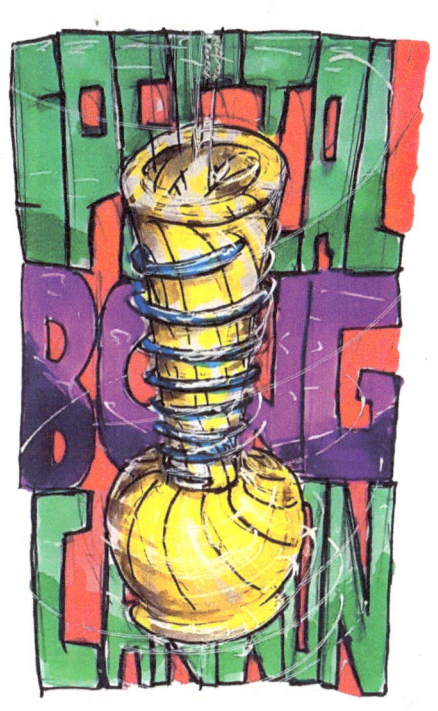
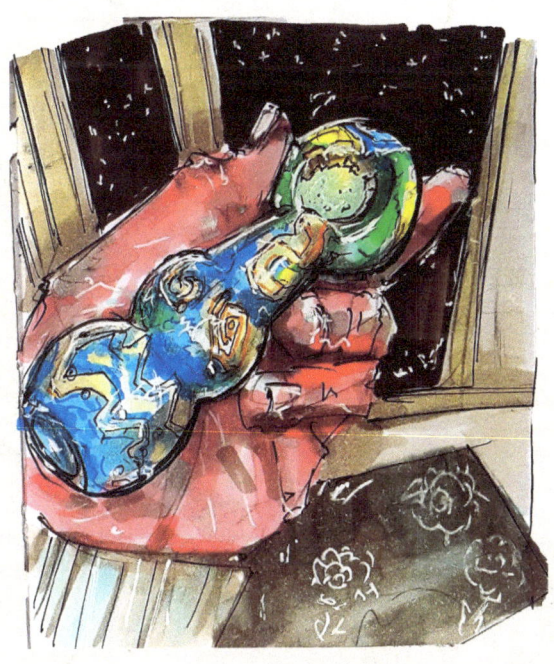

—Tree Watching vol.0—

THE NOT RIGHT SIDE-UP

▲**138** I Was laying on my back listening to music at a 10 and saw this really weird perspective of part of my parents house!
—/u/ryanc69

MAPLE

▲**457** Every time I clean this I need to take a pic of it.
—/u/█████

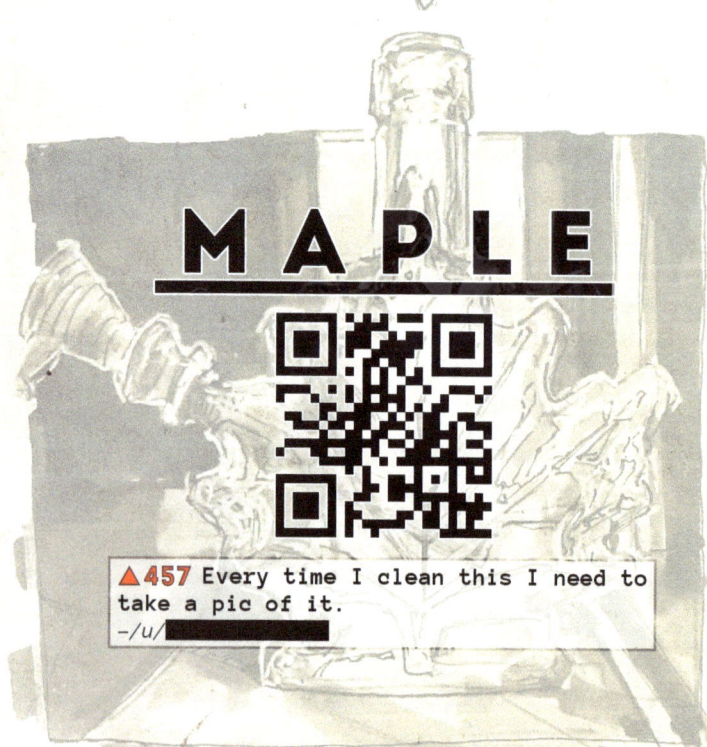

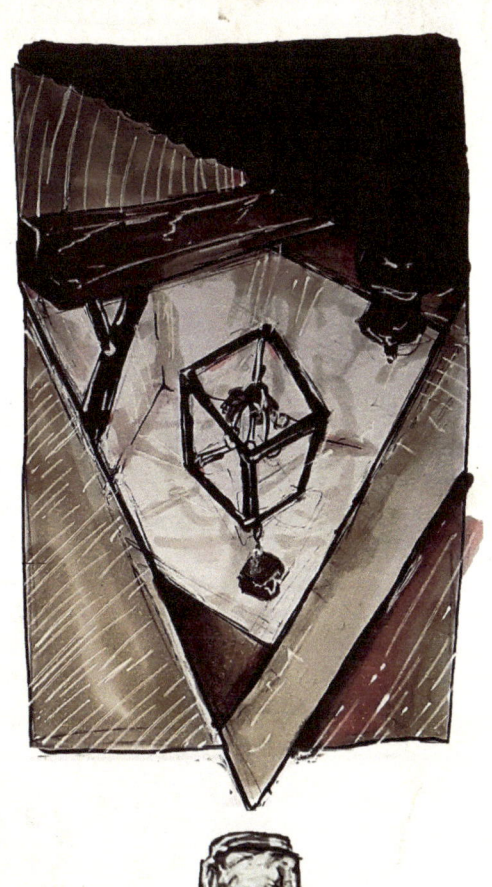

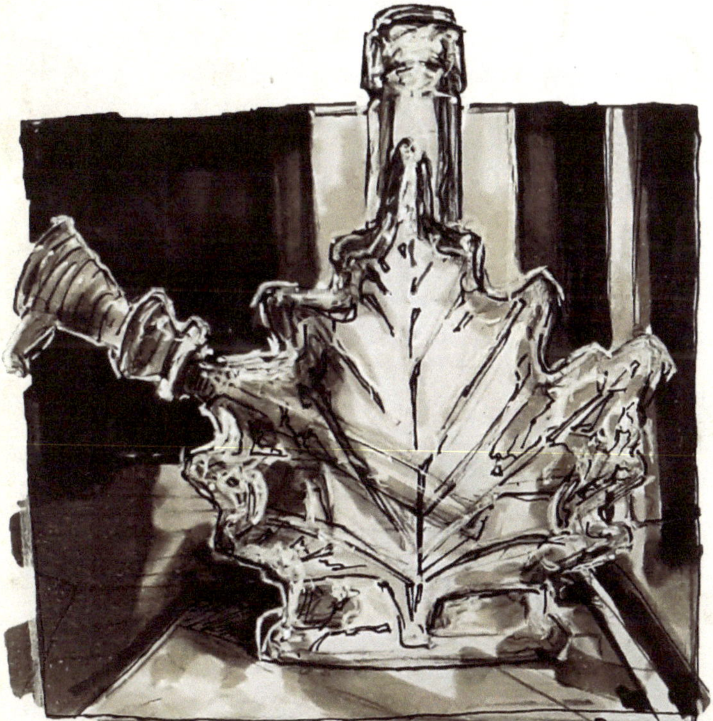

−Tree Watching vol.0−

CHOP CHOP

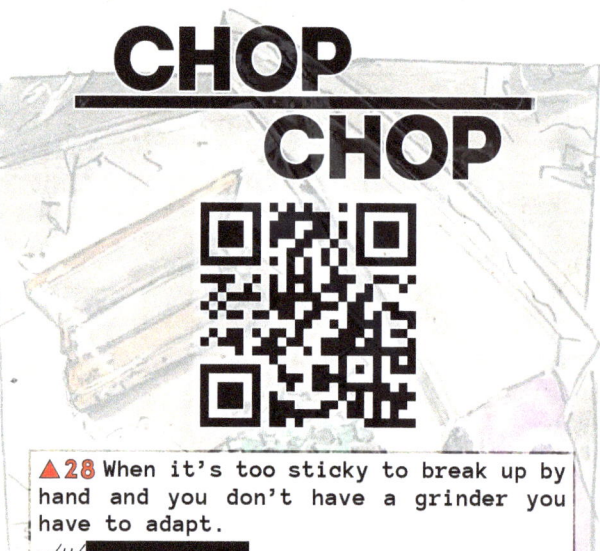

▲28 When it's too sticky to break up by hand and you don't have a grinder you have to adapt.
−/u/▇▇▇▇▇▇

SPIRIT BOWL

▲457 I got the devastating news from my doctor today. I have testicular cancer. I am so, so, so scared. But I'm going to FIGHT this. So smoke up with me, ents, send some positive vibes my way, and keep in mind just how unpredictable life is.
−/u/▇▇▇▇▇▇

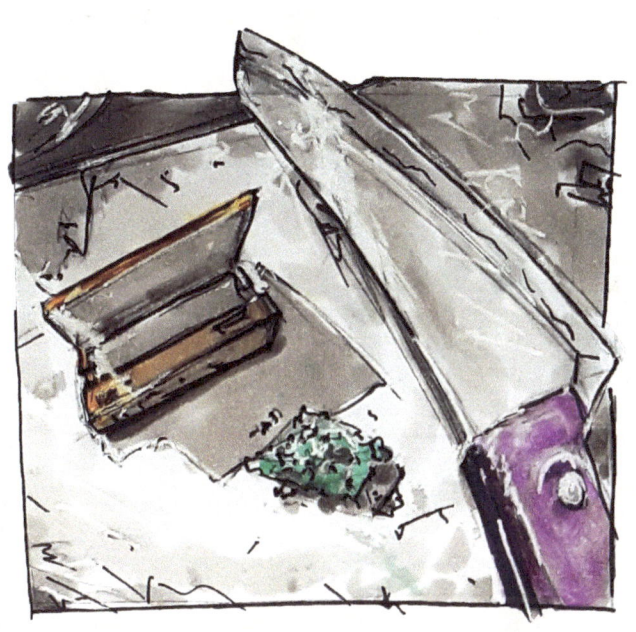

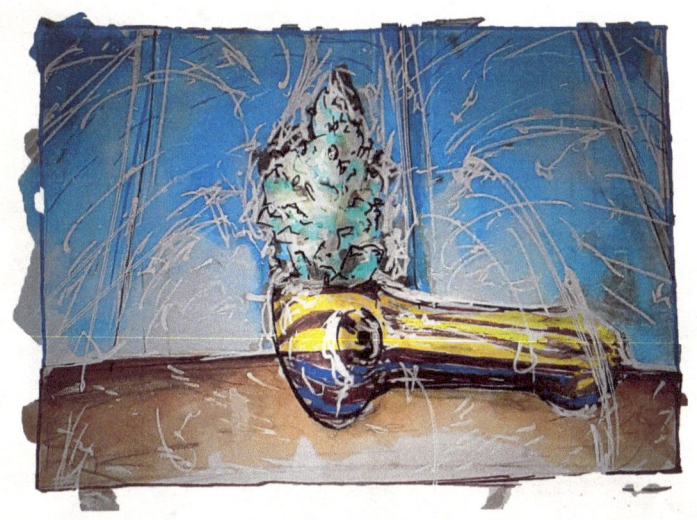

—Tree Watching vol.0—

OH, FUCK
Y   E   S

▲124 Guys I'm 10/10 why did no one tell me I could use a pot for my cereal
—/u/alsknthndrfk

STRAWBERRY
BERRY
BERRY

▲201 Got some Strawberry Kush today. What you guys think?
—/u/▮▮▮▮▮▮▮▮▮

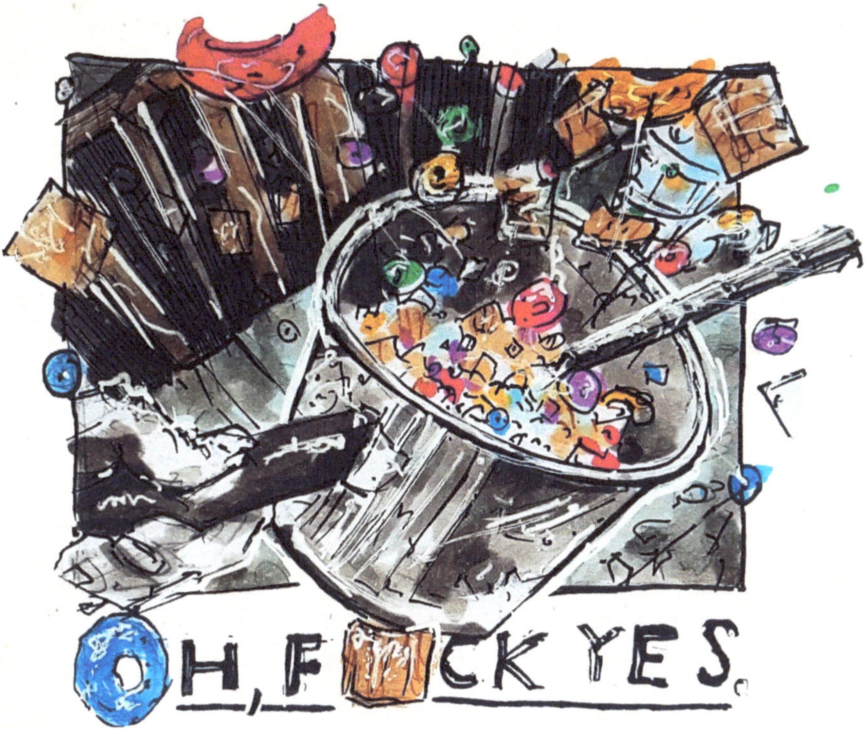

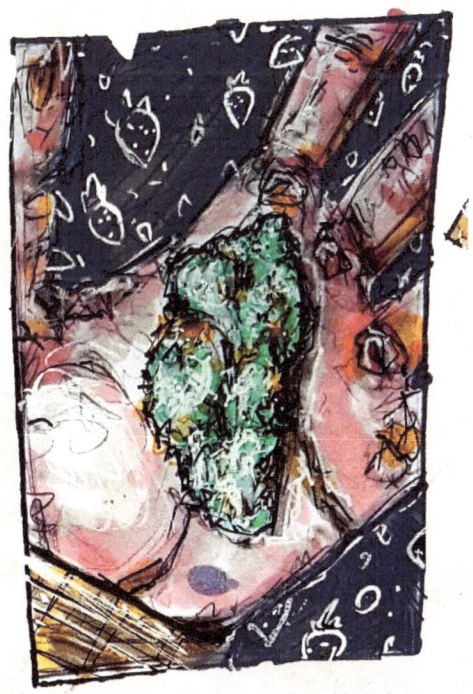

-Tree Watching vol.0-

MAGMA

▲49 It's been a Monday, that's for sure. [6]
-/u/mrtimeywimey

THE MIDNIGHT CARVER

▲517 Carved this at a [6] last night
-/u/Hexadecimated

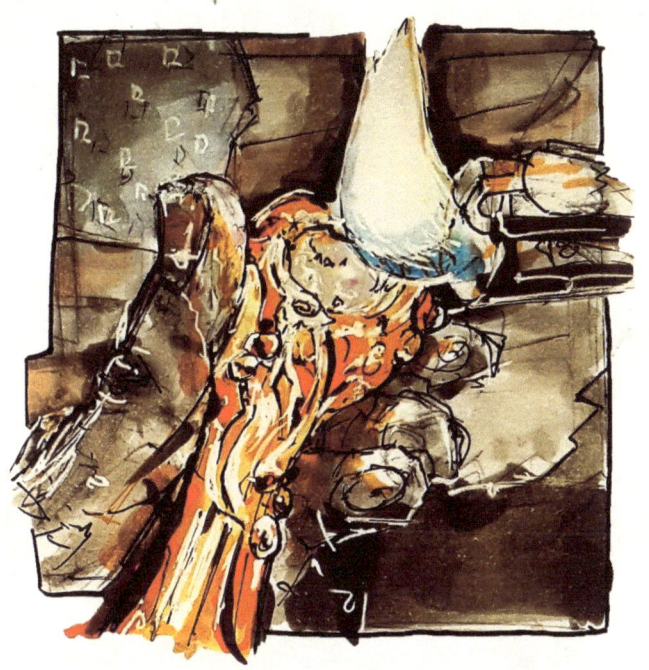
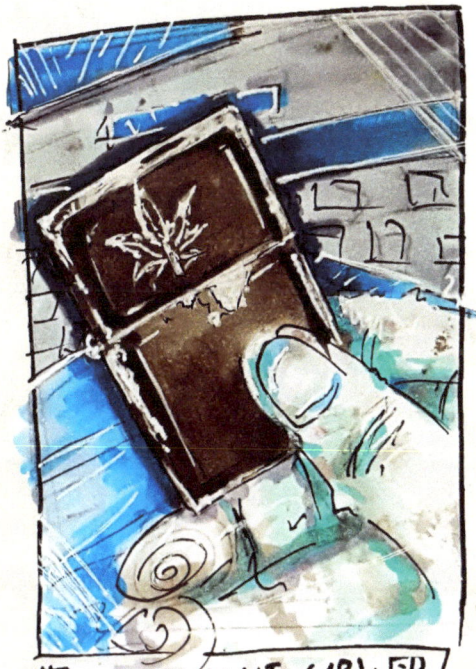

THE MIDNIGHT CARVER!

-Tree Watching vol.0-

HUHIATUS

▲2.0K My girlfriend caught a picture of my reaction to smoking medical oil again after a 2 month hiatus. [14]
-/u/Johnsnoz

RAIN

▲22 Rain
-/u/CharmingToTheCore(Seth Royals)

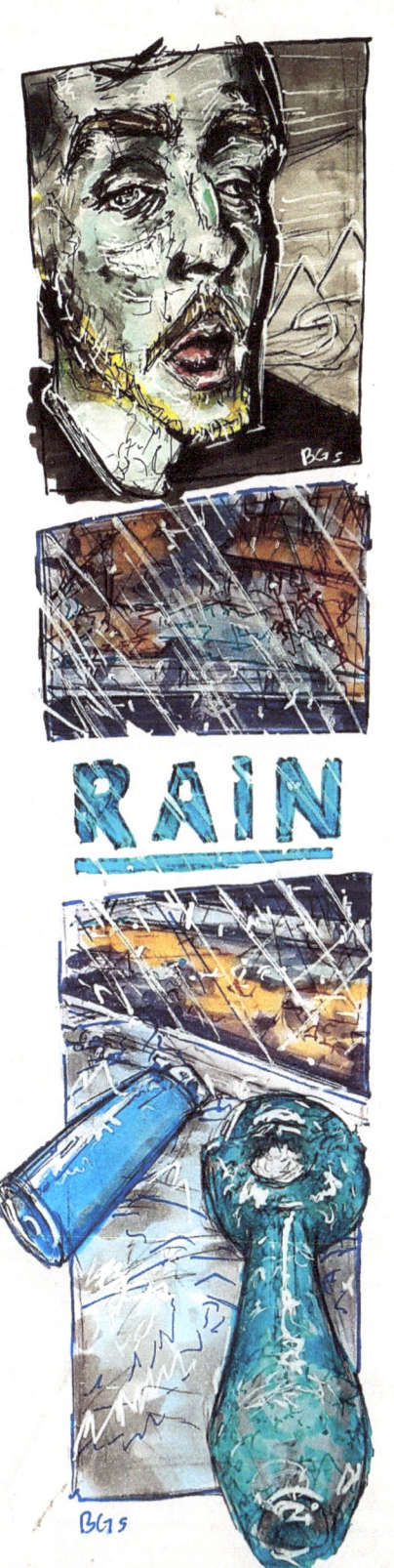

-Tree Watching vol.0-

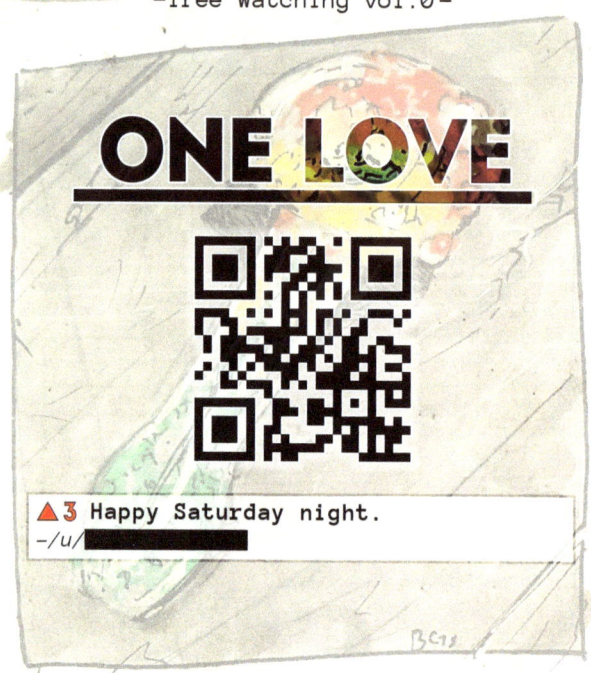

▲3 Happy Saturday night.
-/u/█████

▲1.8K It's █████ in my country and this is the biggest bud I've ever seen
-/u/█████

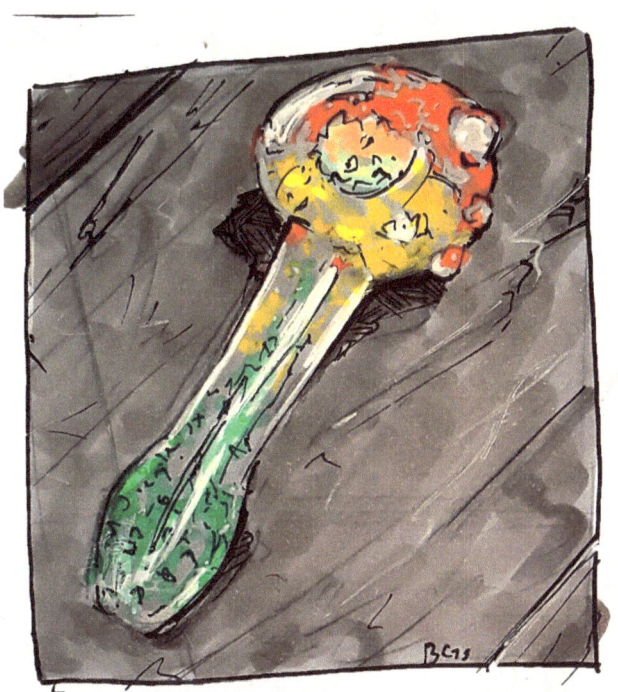
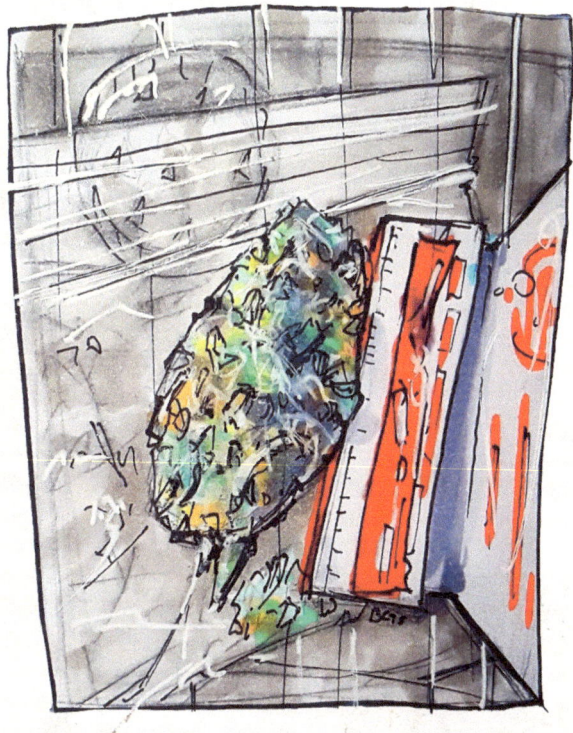

—Tree Watching vol.0—

SOUR CANDY

▲123 [I was cleaning the garage today and found my lava lamp. 4]
—/u/MarijuanaMuppet

TOKIN TOKEN

▲33 Found this cool arcade token one day, been in there ever since.
—/u/xXDrewBloodXx

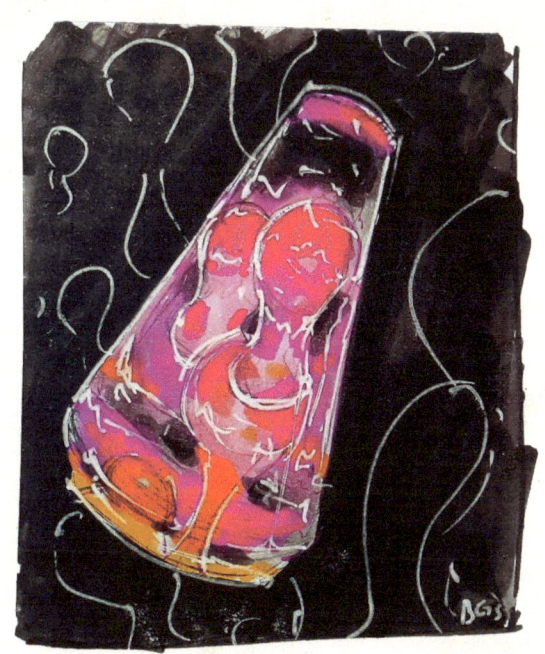

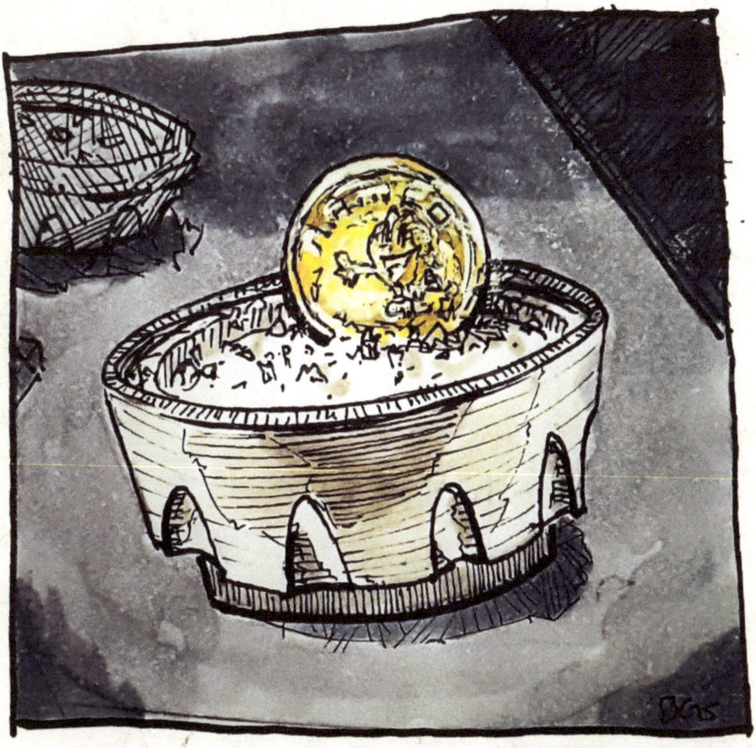

−Tree Watching vol.0−

▲7.9K My favorite holiday tradition. We call it Marijuanukkah.
−/u/SonicTitan303

▲219 Smoke spot atop a volcano crater, Mount Liamuiga, St. Kitts.
−/u/zeapups

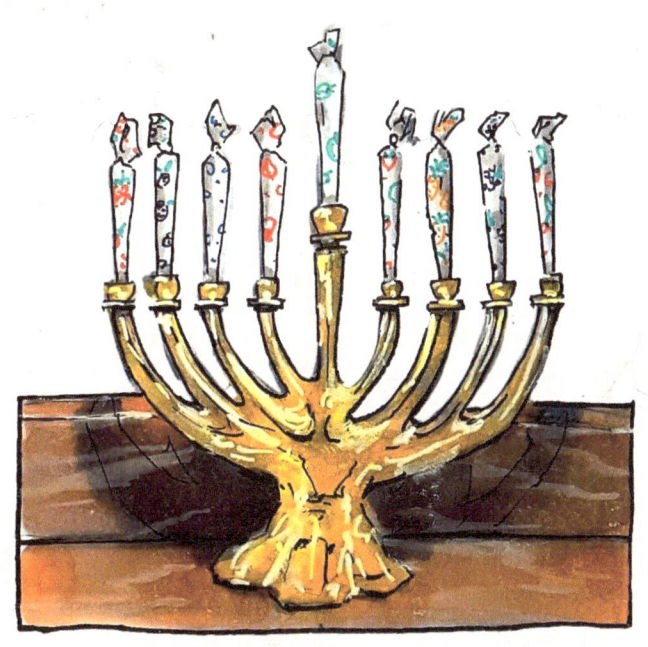
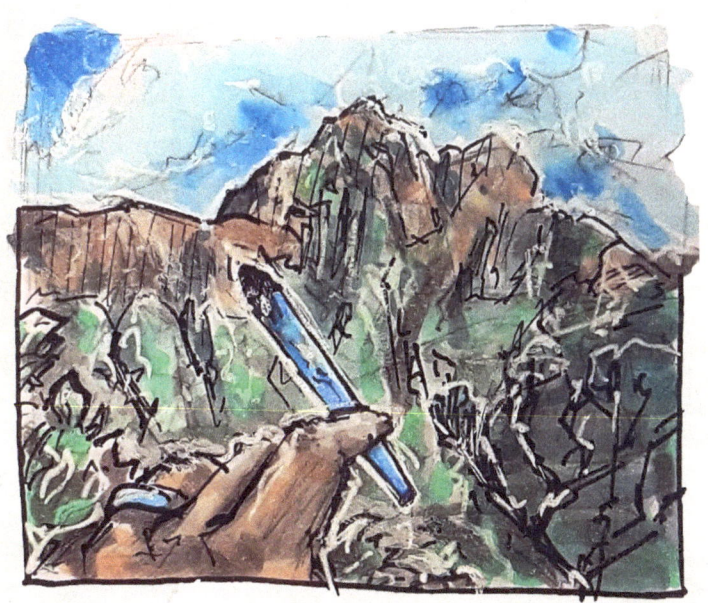

-Tree Watching vol.0-

TOMATO
PLANT

▲3.4K Me next to my dad's tomato plant, circa 1994
-/u/turdfergisin

THIS TOMATO PLANT SMELLS FUNNY.

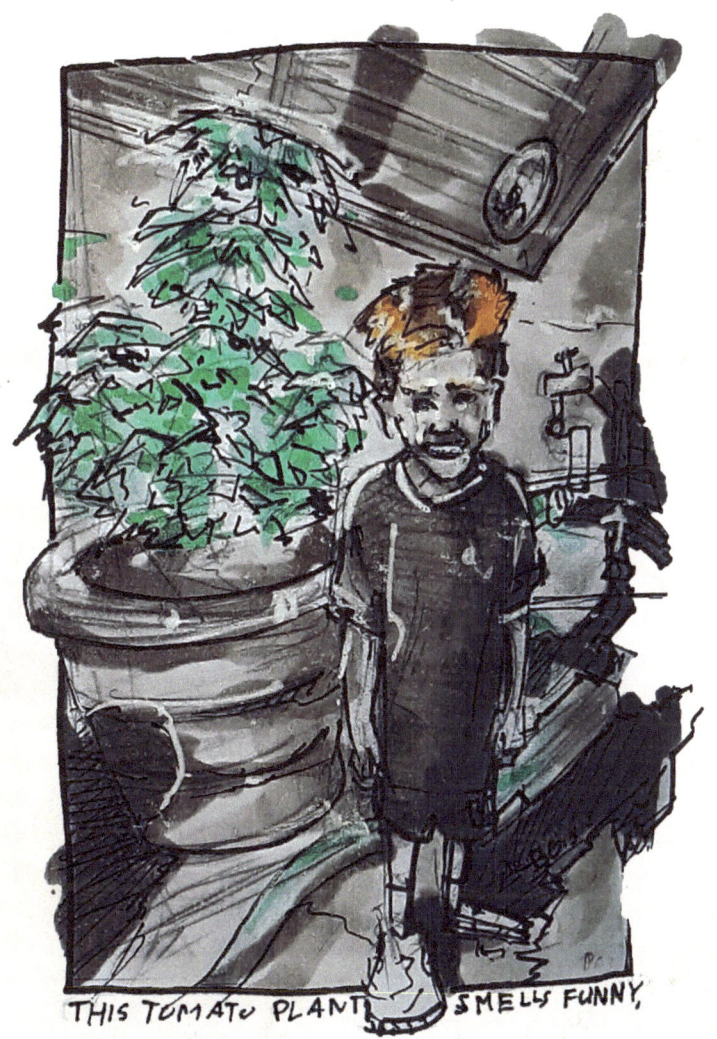

-Tree Watching vol.0-

CLYPNO
CAT

▲288 Got a lighter to match my pipe
-/u/RysGottaFly

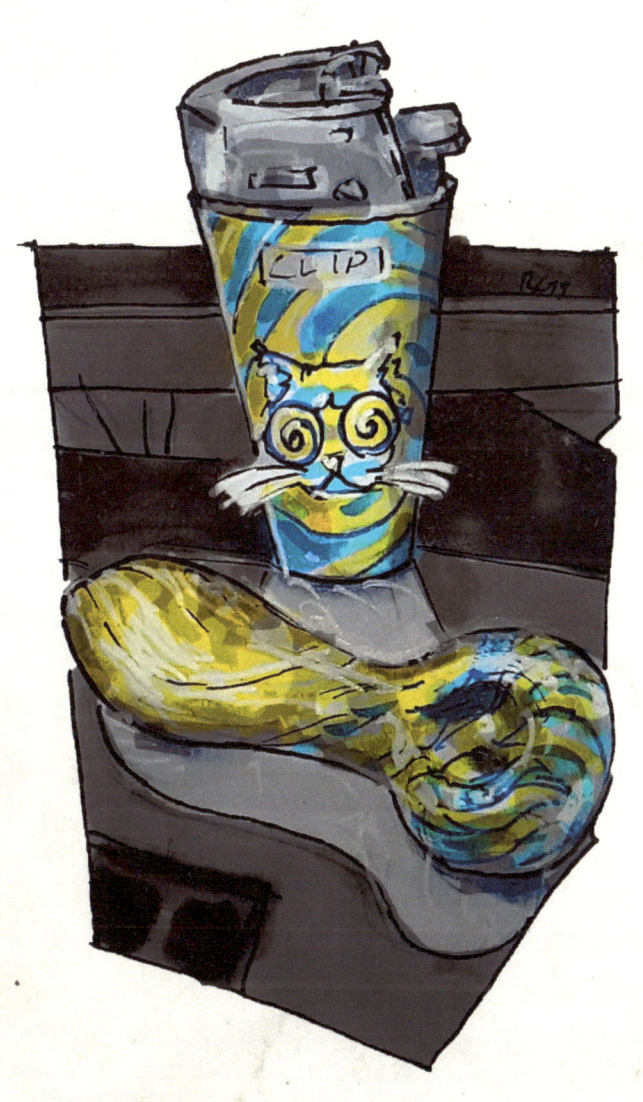

—Tree Watching vol.0—

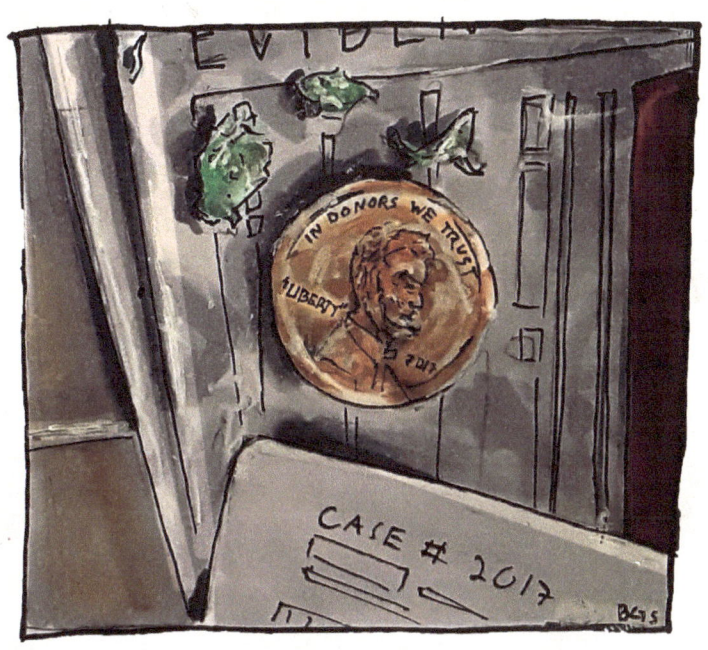

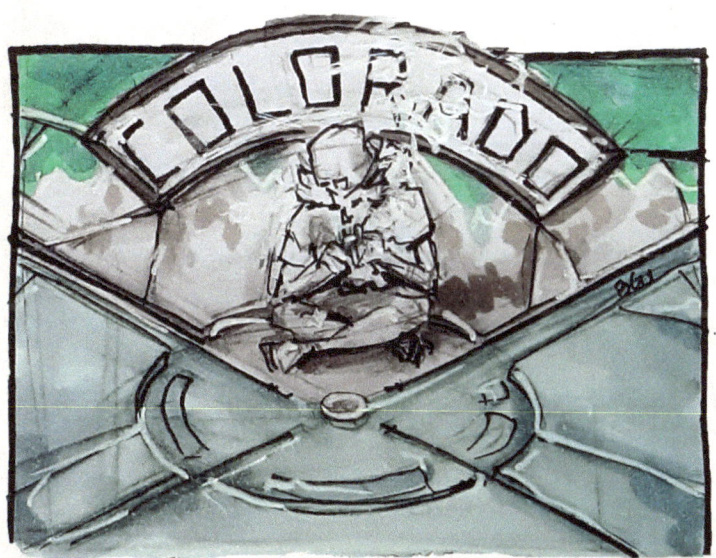

COME FOR THE EVERYTHING, STAY FOR THE EVERYTHING

-Tree Watching vol.0-

▲70 Small town memories
-/u/DeltaDiezel

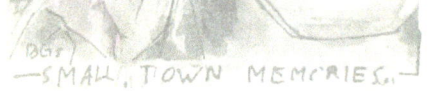

▲219 After being dankrupt for weeks.
Couldn't be happier. One of us!!!!
-/u/pmt666

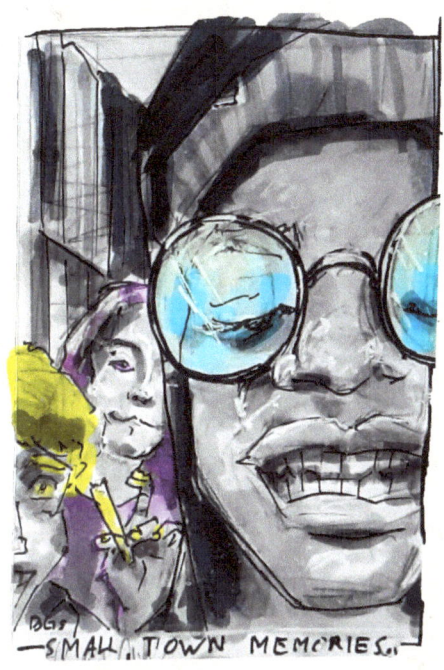
—SMALL TOWN MEMORIES—

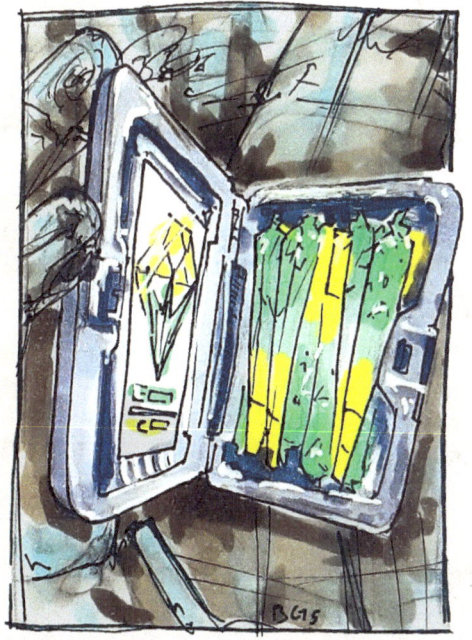

-Tree Watching vol.0-

▲388 White Widow x Forbidden Fruit
-/u/Cjcoltellino

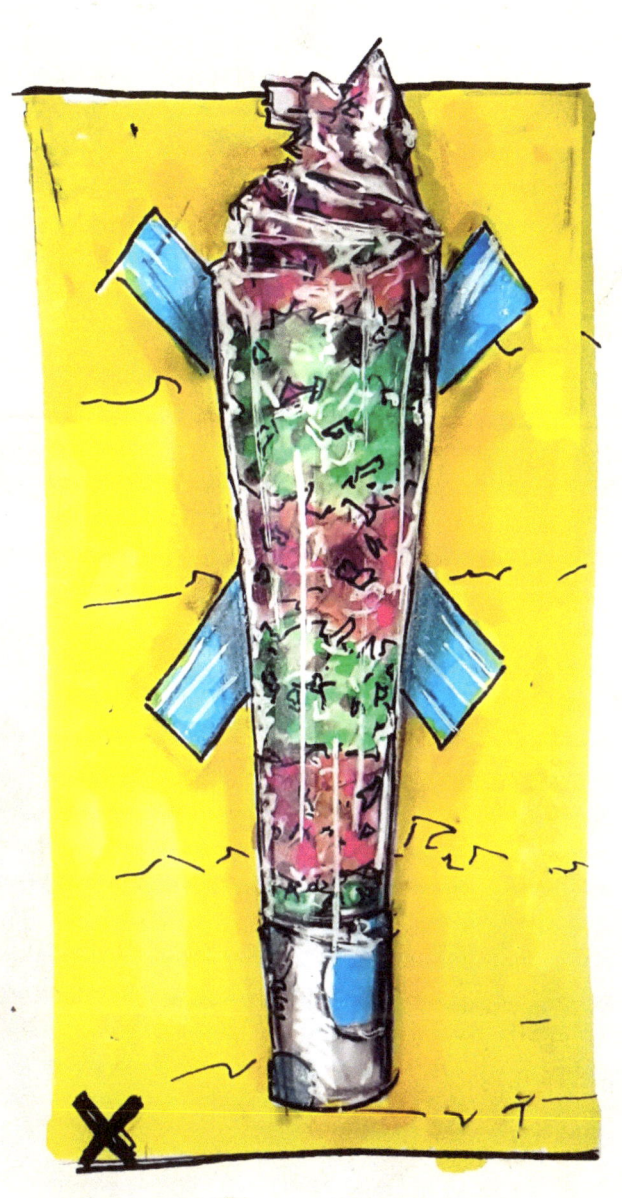

-Tree Watching vol.0-

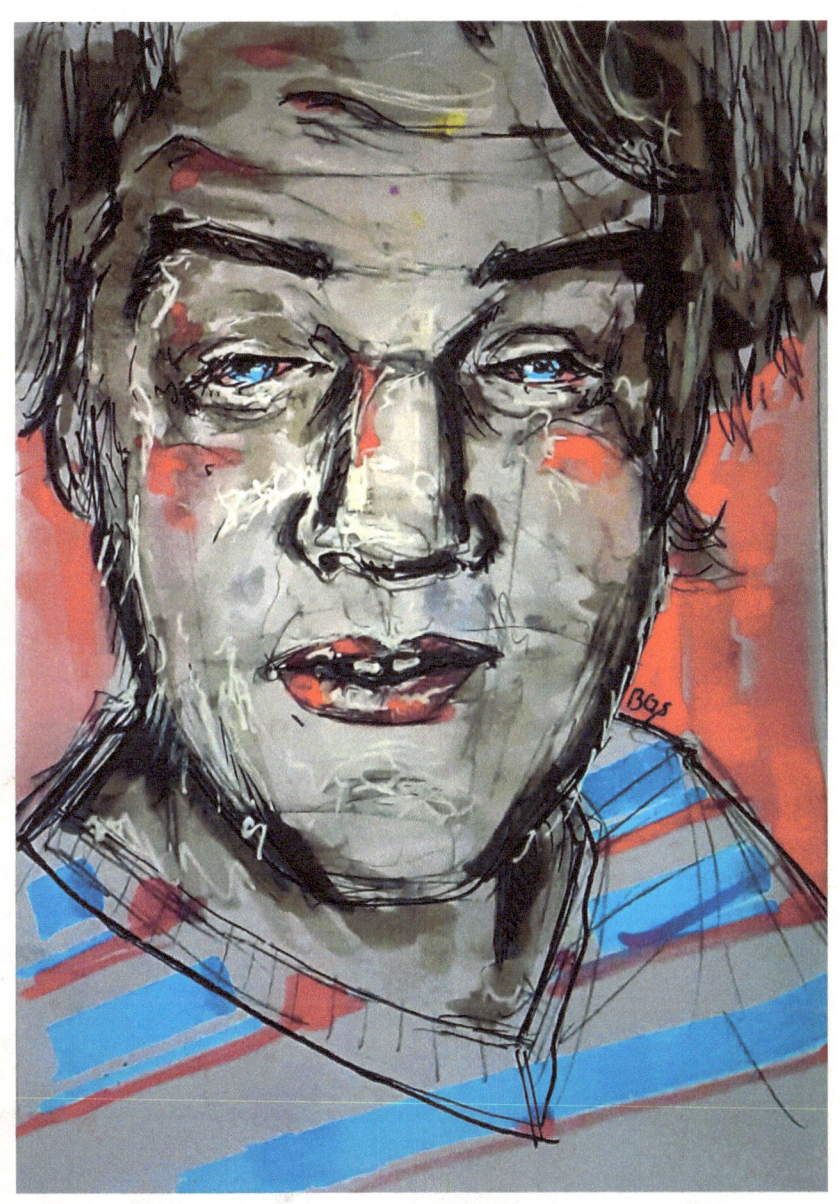

THE INDEX

[*QR Codes* are for the reddit profile post of each illustration and feature a **link to the reference**, any **user discussion**, and links to purchase the illustration on **stickers, prints, *and more*.**]

-INDEX-

I.1

BLUE GLEEPSTONE
[P.-]

GDP/LJ
[P.2]

Early Christmas
[P.2]

SIDE EFFECT.
[P.4]

TIS THE SEASON
[P.4]

JAMBI
[P.6]

THICC
[P.6]

D.A.R.T.
[P.8]

CLEAN GLASS
[P.8]

Zen Garden
[P.10]

A Great Cafe
[P.10]

EUREKA !!!!!!!!!!!!!!!!
[P.12]

Heart
[P.12]

SOLO DOLO
[P.12]

On The Go
[P.14]

First Grow
[P.16]

Perfect Pair
[P.16]

WITCHCRAFT
[P.18]

I.2 −INDEX−

Garden Variety

[P.18]

Atlantean Beetle

[P.18]

Happy Thanksgiving!

[P.20]

Dessert

[P.20]

BAKE THE TURKEY

[P.20]

WUMBO

[P.22]

Little Blue
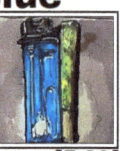
[P.22]

RAZZ 2.0

[P.24]

Water Spots

[P.24]

Special Bong Cannon
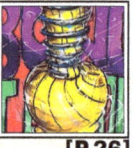
[P.26]

Squiggly Bits

[P.26]

The Not Right Side Up

[P.28]

Maple

[P.28]

Chop Chop

[P.30]

Spirit Bowl
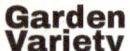
[P.30]

Oh, Fuck Yes

[P.32]

STRAWBERRY BERRY BERRY

[P.32]

Magma

[P.34]

—INDEX— I.3

The Midnight Carver

[P.34]

Huhiatus

[P.36]

RAIN
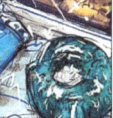
[P.36]

One Love

[P.38]

Fruit Punch

[P.38]

Sour Candy

[P.40]

Tokin Token

[P.40]

Happy Marijuanukkah!

[P.42]

With A View
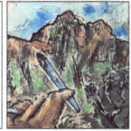
[P.42]

Tomato Plant

[P.44]

Clypno Cat

[P.46]

Evidence
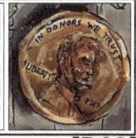
[P.48]

Colorado

[P.48]

Small Town Memories

[P.50]

EMERALD

[P.50]

White Widow X Forbidden Fruit

[P.52]

HUH
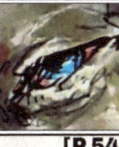
[P.54]

www.ingramcontent.com/pod-product-compliance
Lightning Source LLC
Chambersburg PA
CBHW040325220526
45473CB00009B/2578